What do you see?

An adventure in illustration

By Jessica Wheadon

2015

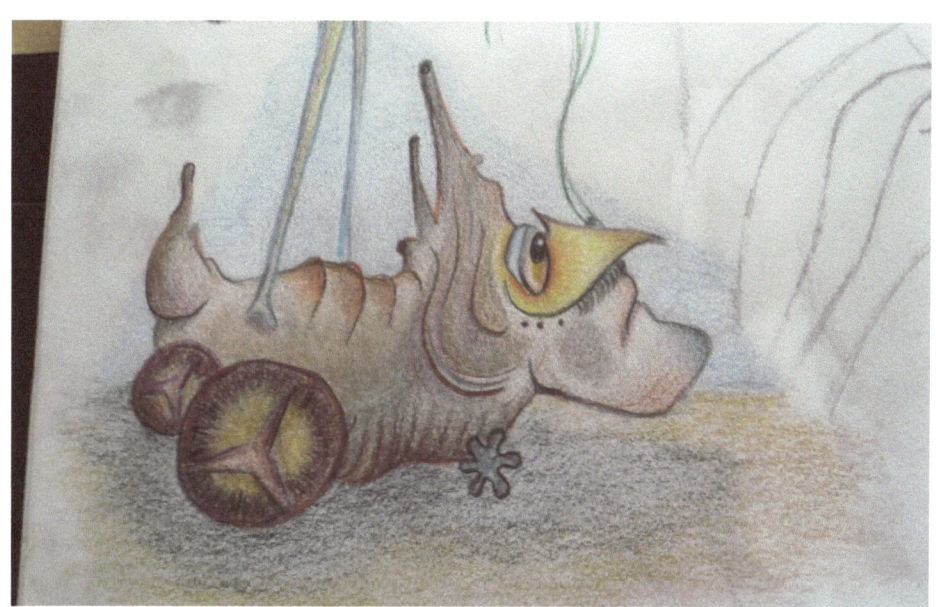

A child's ride on toy – J.Wheadon

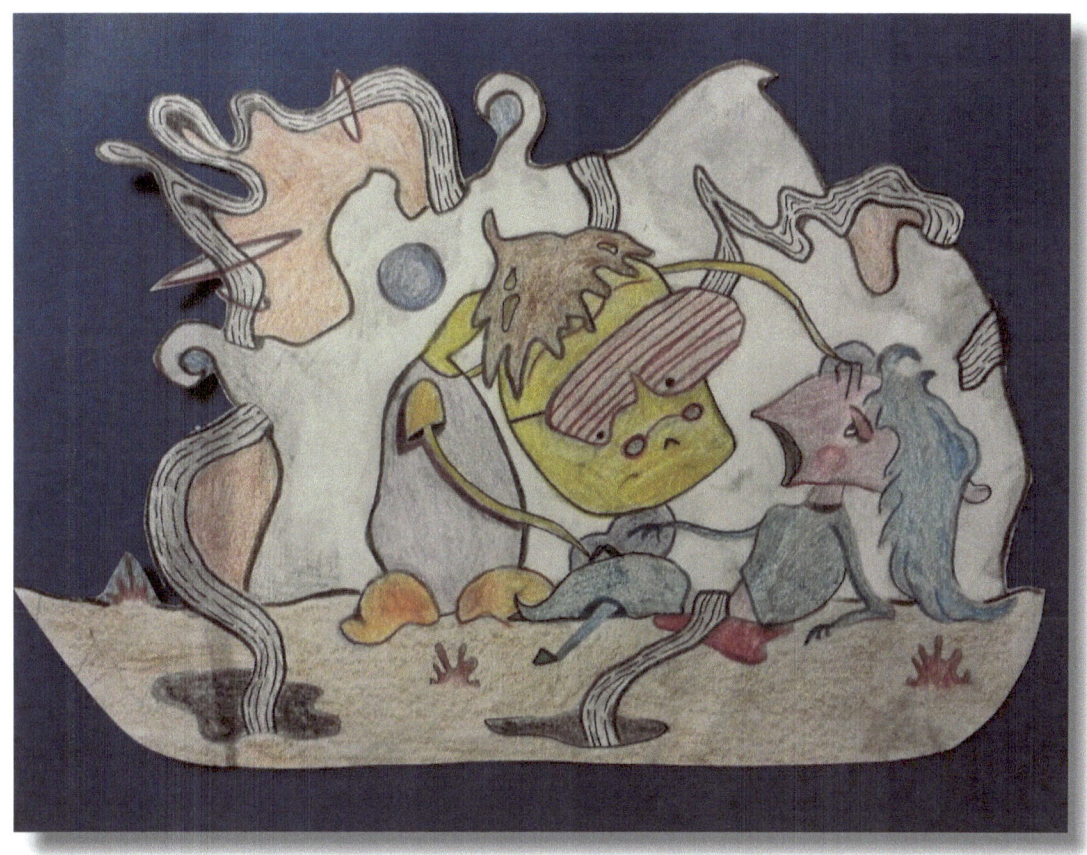

What do you see in this picture?

I see a lady who has just been run over, and a kind man with red stripy glasses and orange feet who has come to help.

She looks like she is upset. I wonder who ran her over?

I think it would be very difficult to drive in this area, the road is incredibly wonky! Would your car fit into a small hole in the ground? Mine wouldn't.

I hope she feels better soon.

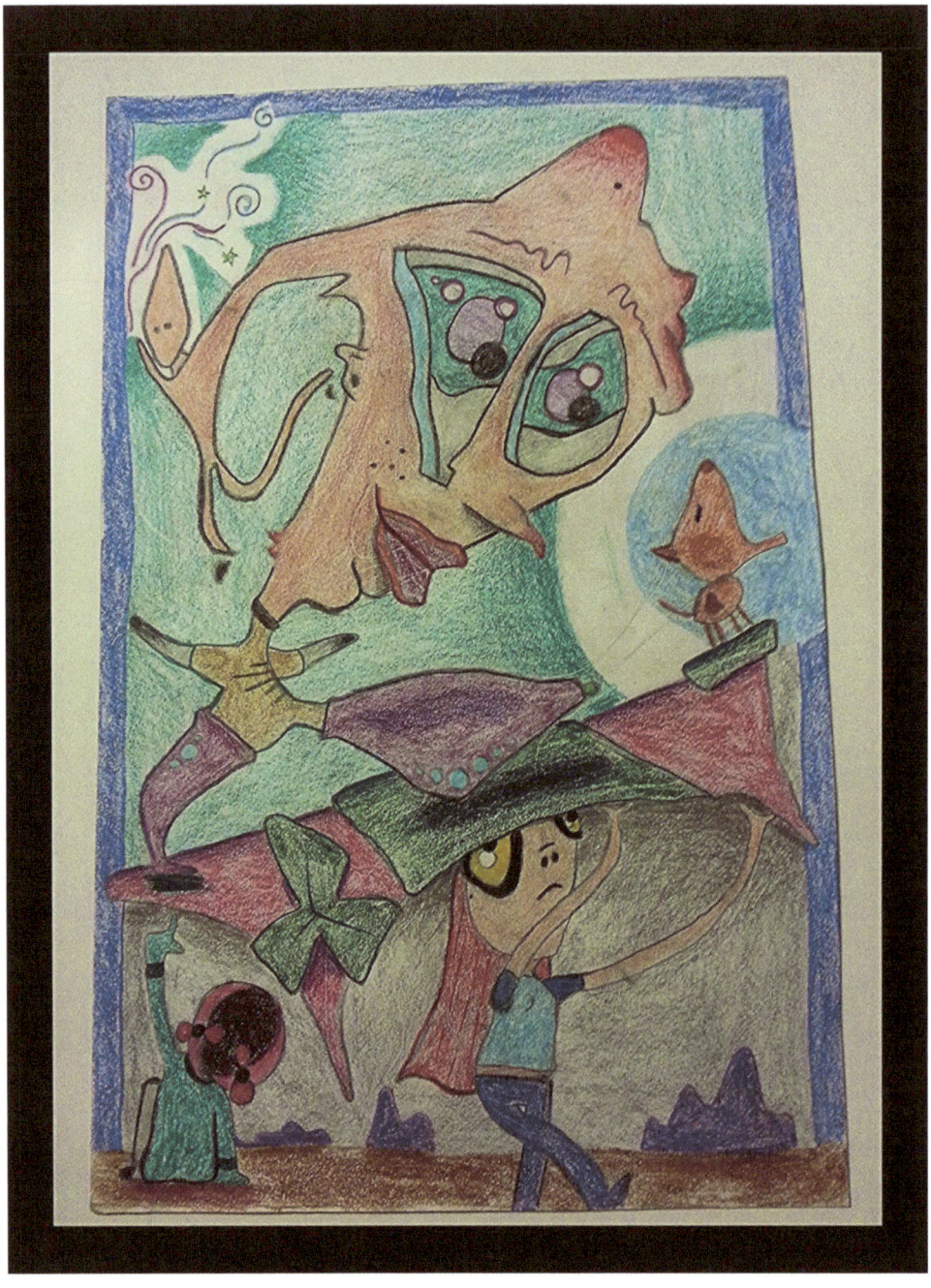

Whatever this picture means I think the girls underneath must be very strong!

I think the man is going to catch the dog, perhaps his howling is bothering the neighbours.

Nothing can possibly explain the fact that he has a dancer attached to his head. What do you think he is for?

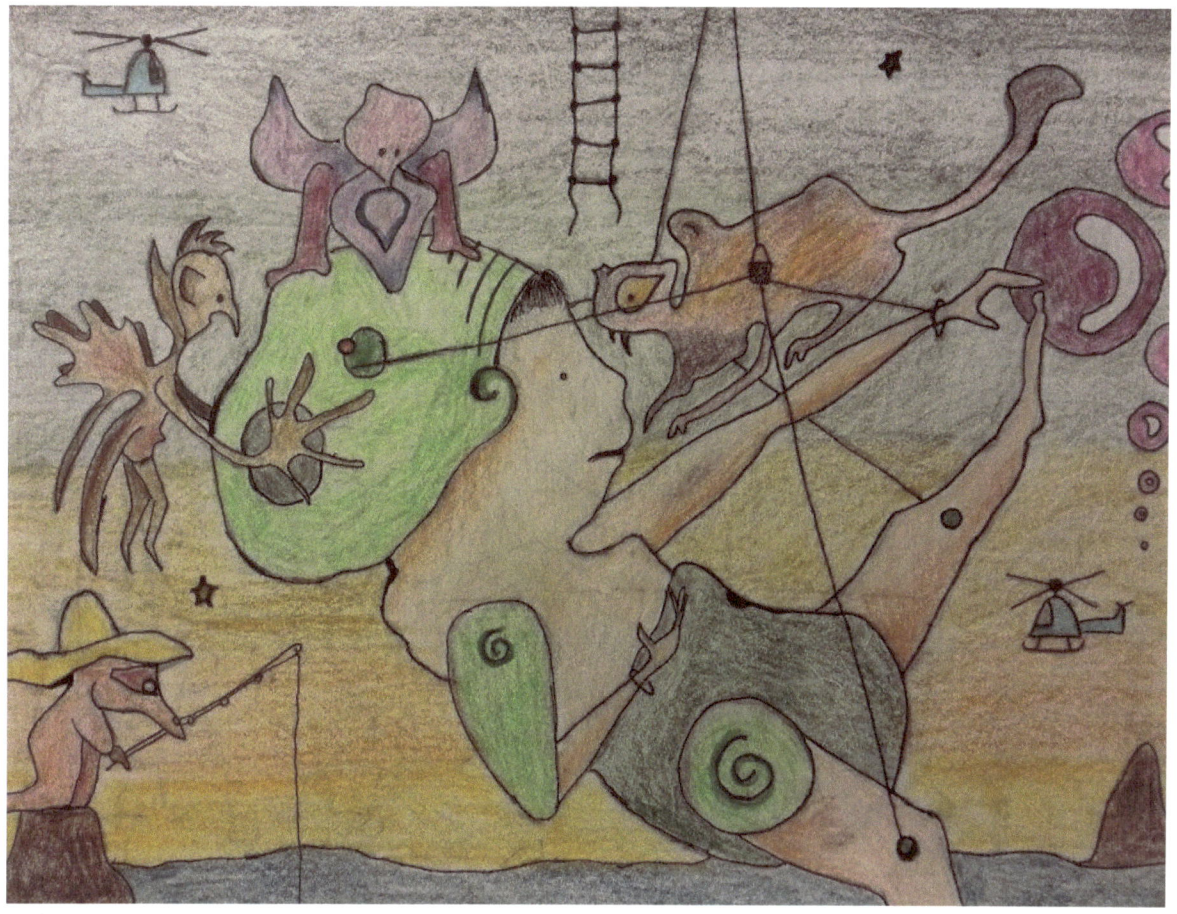

Now what is happening here?

I know, it's a baby factory, and each of those critters are helping to make a baby. Looks like they are nearly done, what do you think they will call him? Or is it a her?

Everyone in the picture looks like they are working very hard except the person in the yellow hat. He seems to be fishing.

I don't think his boss will be very happy!

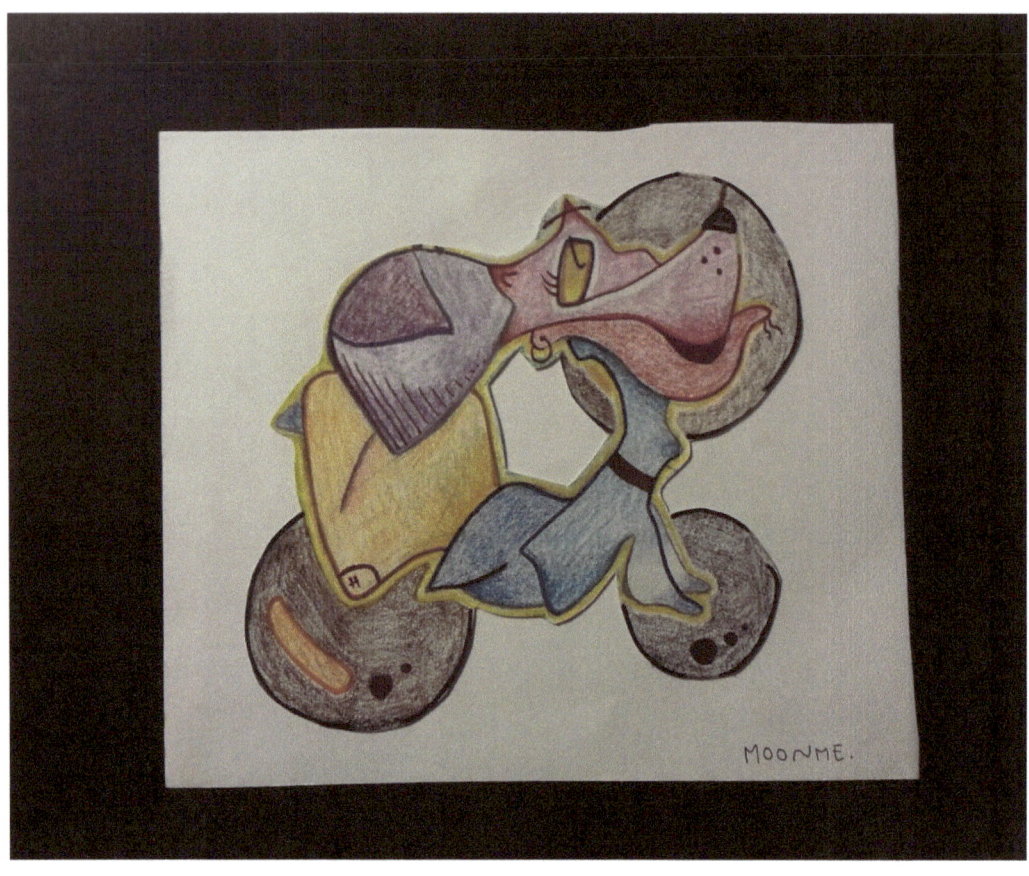

Wow, what do you see here?

I see a dog, who is also a bicycle. His wheels are brown and his ears are purple.

How do you think he became a bike?

I heard somewhere that he was near an explosion, and had been riding his bike at the time. Perhaps they were fused together.

Either way he looks pretty happy. Although now he might have to sleep in the shed.

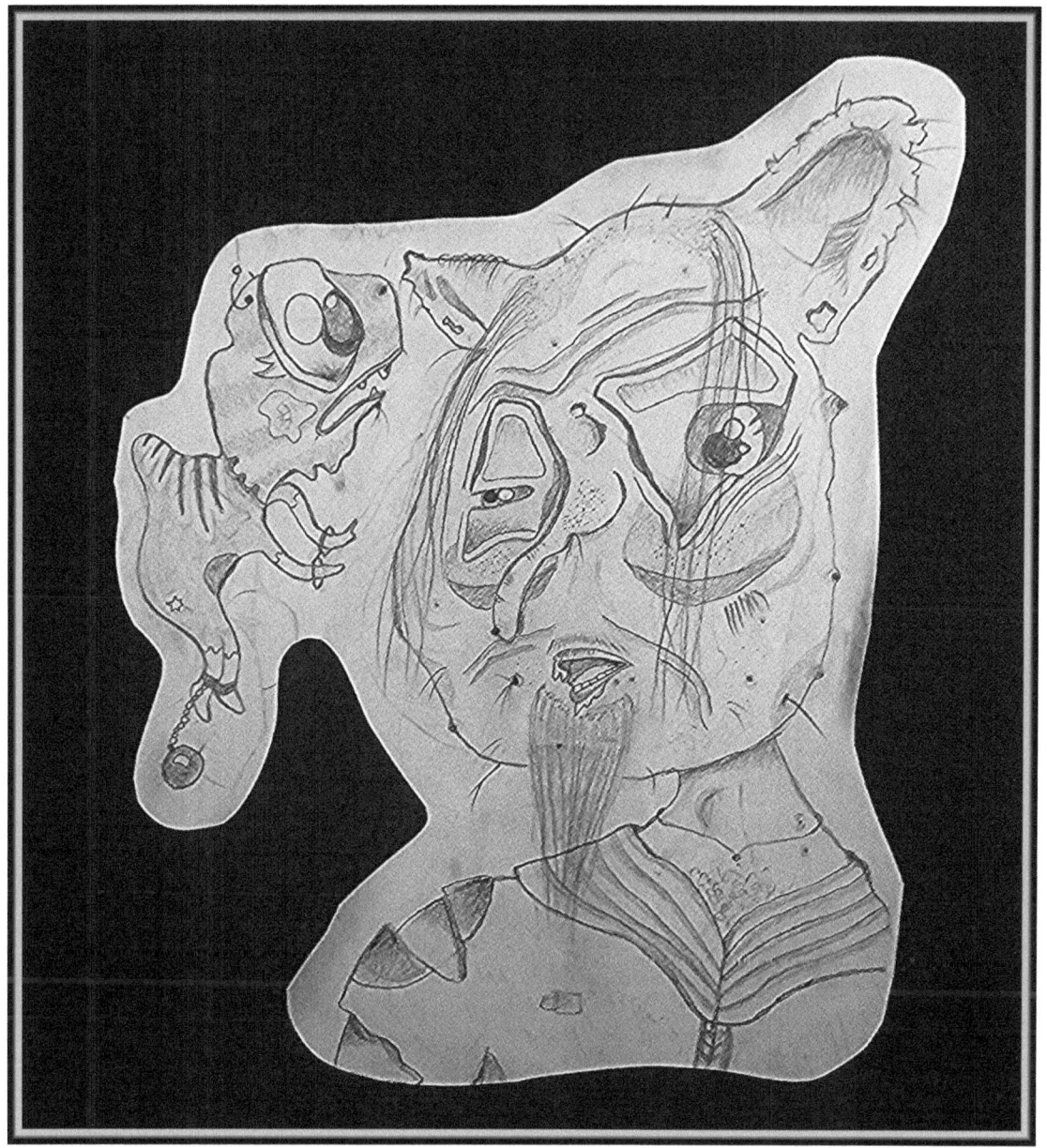

There seems to be some whispering going on here, the little animal appears to be talking into the ear of someone very tired.

I wonder what he is saying, and why does he have a ball and chain attached to his ankle?

I wouldn't entirely trust him, his eyes are far too big.

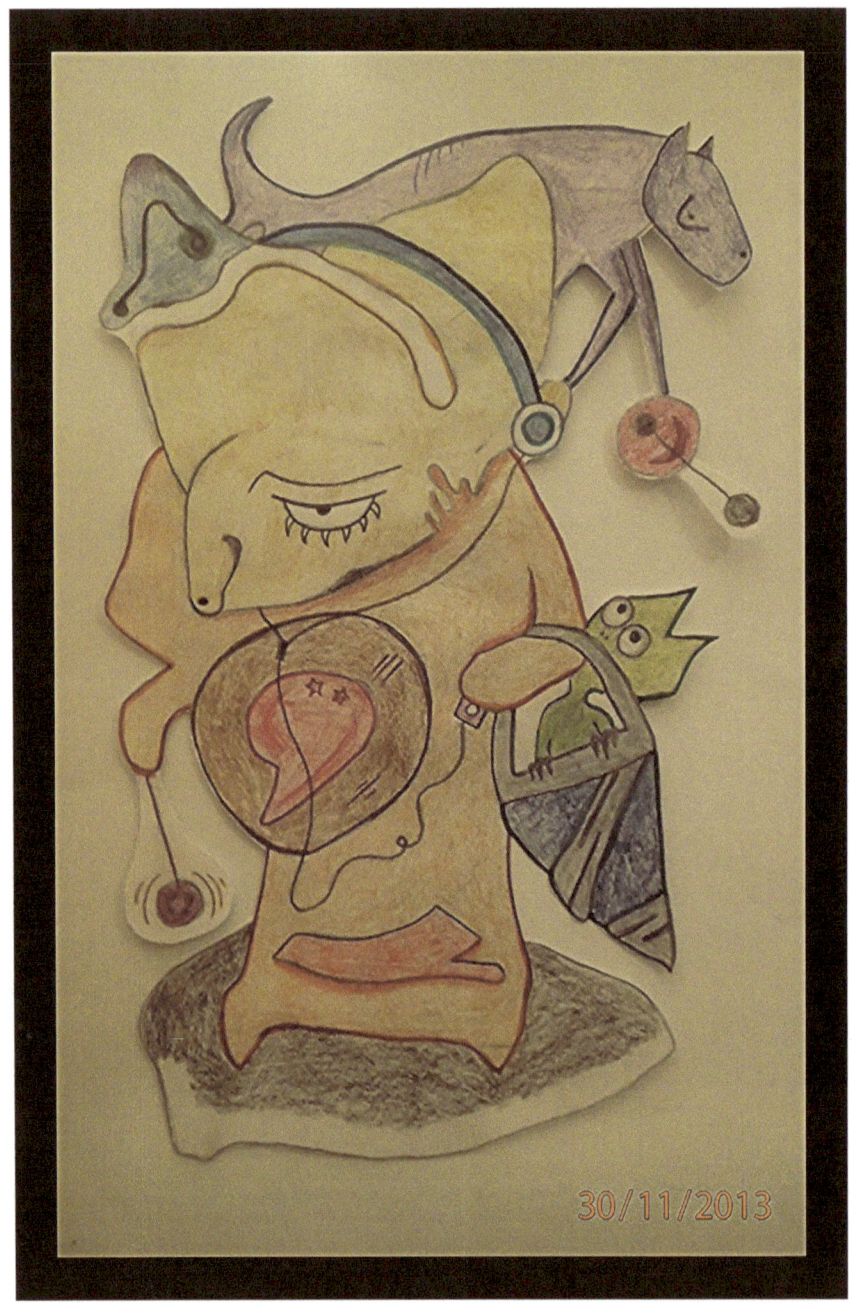

30/11/2013

The things that first jump out at me when I look at this picture are:

A yo-yo, a green alien in a handbag, a purple dog and blue headphones.

Can you spot all these things?

What can you see that I missed?

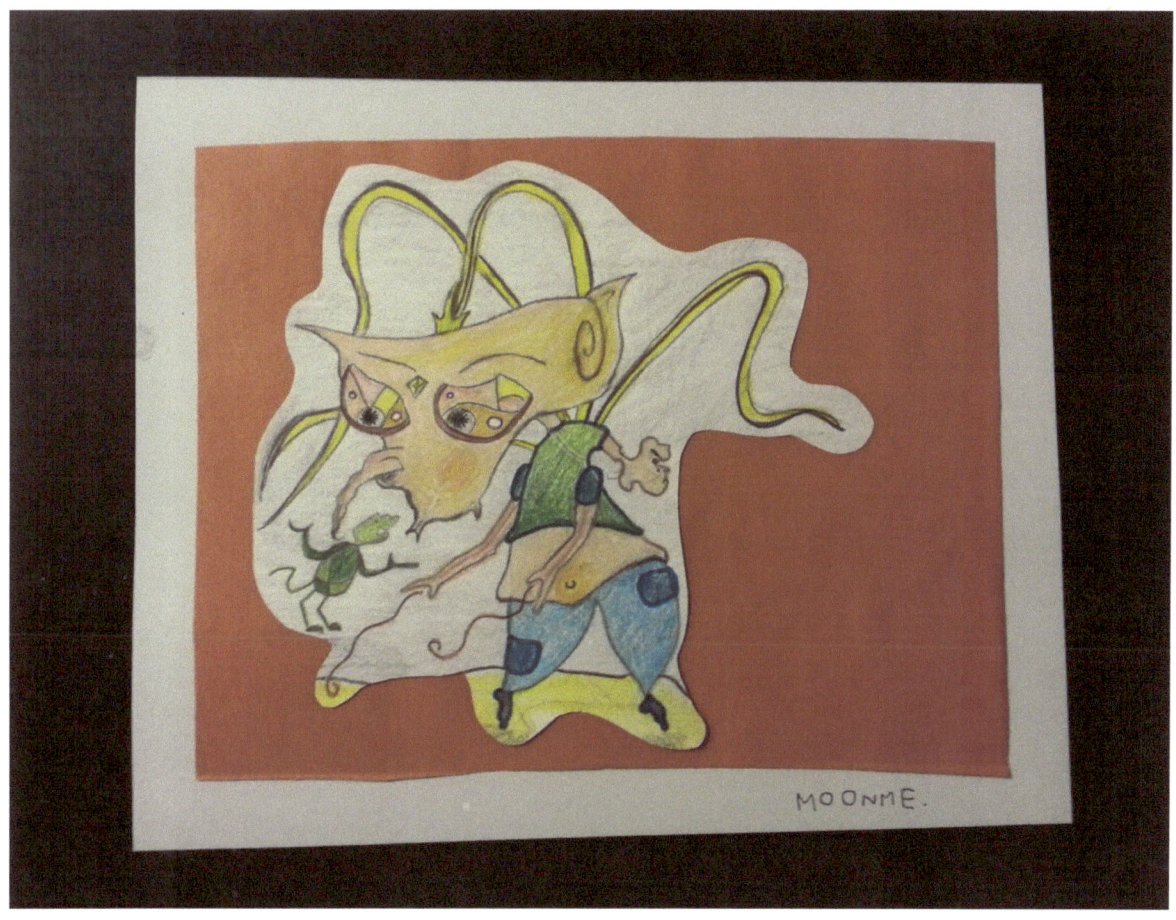

I'm interested to know what you see here.

I see an alien, with tentacles coming out of his back who is talking to a turtle.

The turtle must be very clever, he is standing on the air!

I think the alien needs to pull his pants up, or pull his shirt down – what do you think?

I can see his belly button!

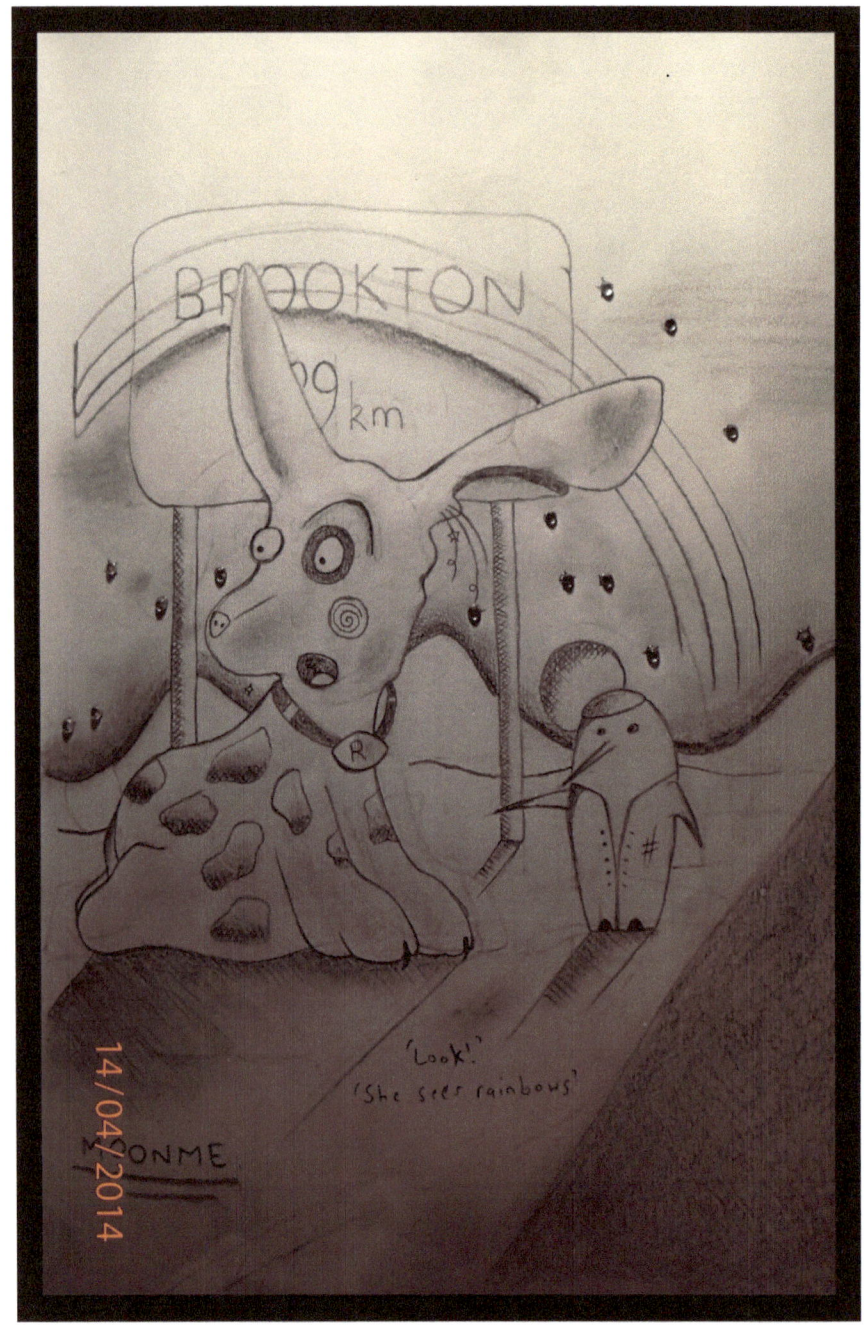

This must be an old world, it is black and white.

I think the figure on the left is a dog, but what is the figure on the right?

There seem to be rainbows in a place called Brookton, have you been there before? It is a country town and is surrounded by sheep.

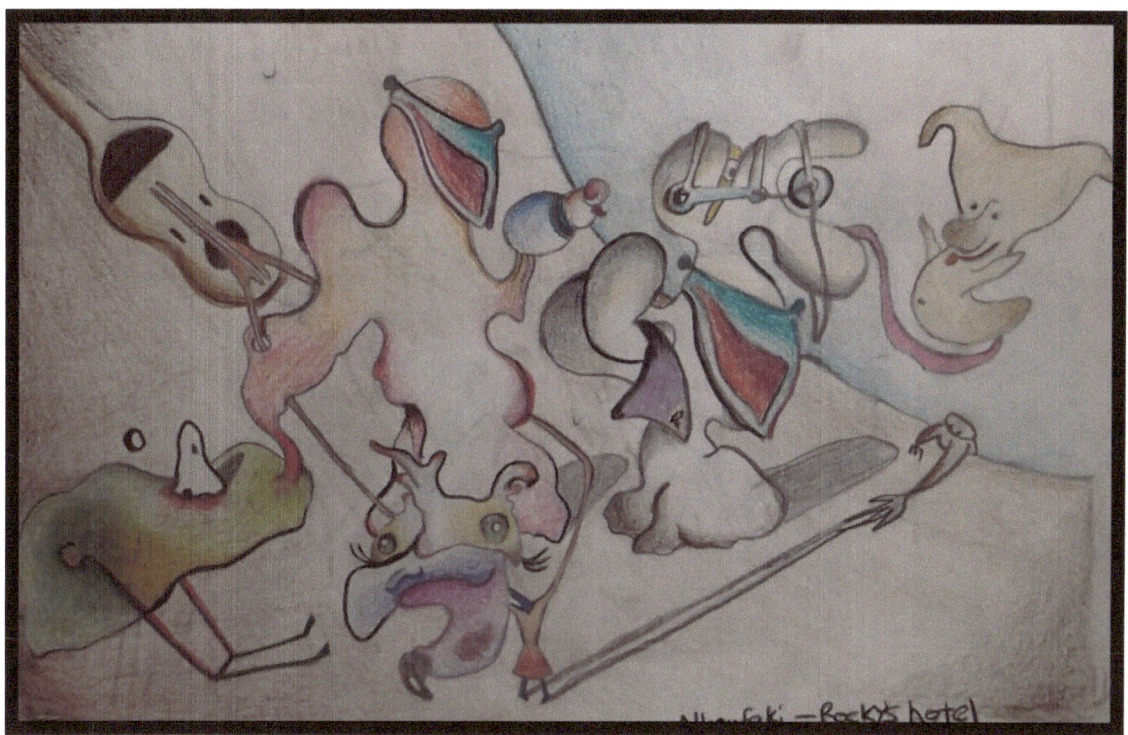

There are lots of characters in this one. What do you think they are doing?

I'll tell you what I think.

On the far right is a dog, he is floating in the air on the edge of a cliff. Four other creatures, including half a camel, a ghost with a gun, a swing monster and someone holding a guitar are following him over the cliff. They are going to a hotel, where you can check out anytime you like, but you can never leave.

Can you see the person crawling up over the edge? He is stealing shadows.

They are a naughty pair, I think.

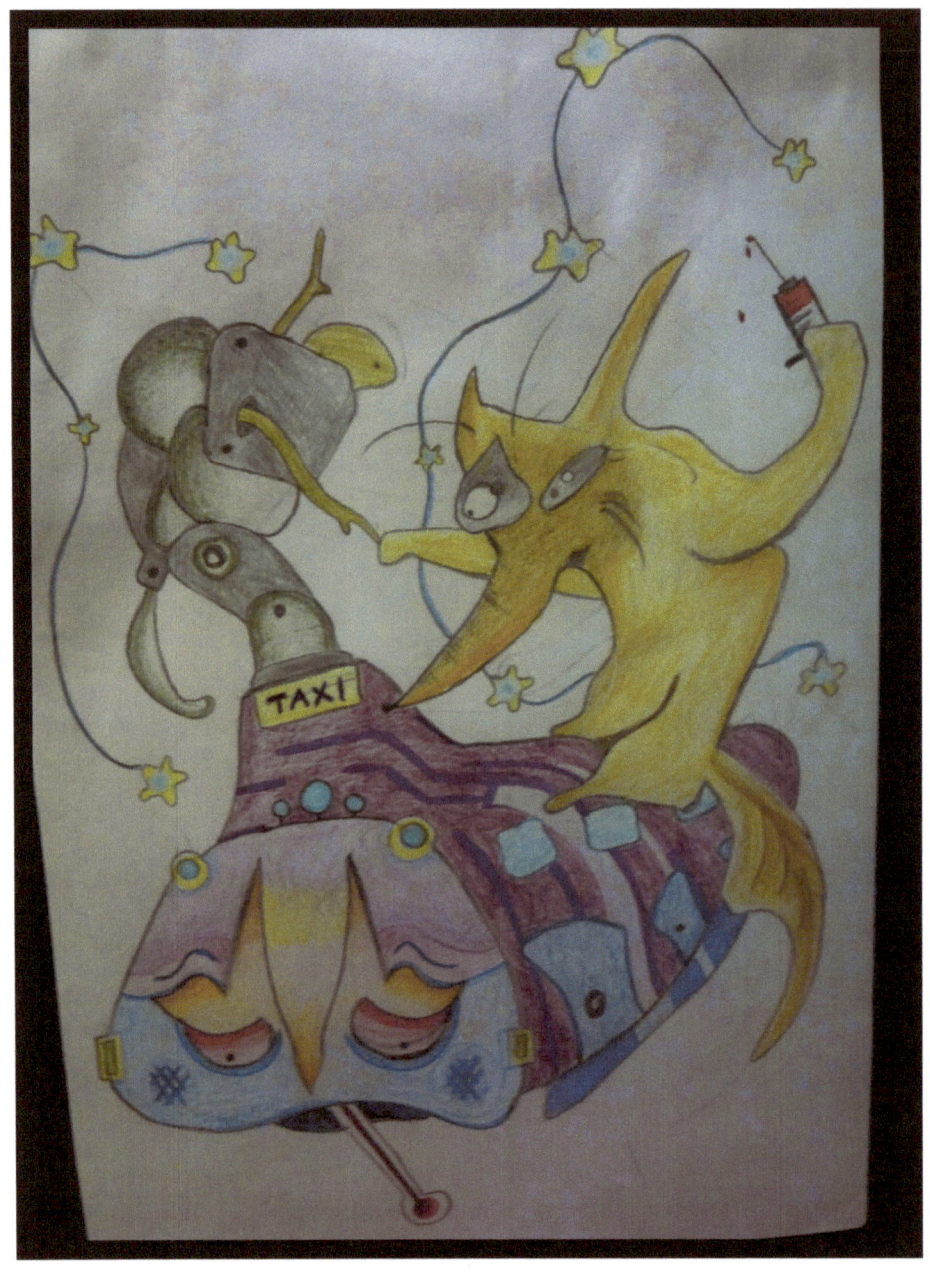

I can see in this picture that someone is sick, can you see who it is?

A taxi? How can a taxi get sick? Would a taxi catch a cold, or the measles?

Thankfully, some friends have come to give him an injection to make him feel better. They may not look very professional but I'm sure they know what they are doing. I mean, who can balance on a wobbly taxi and still give an effective injection?

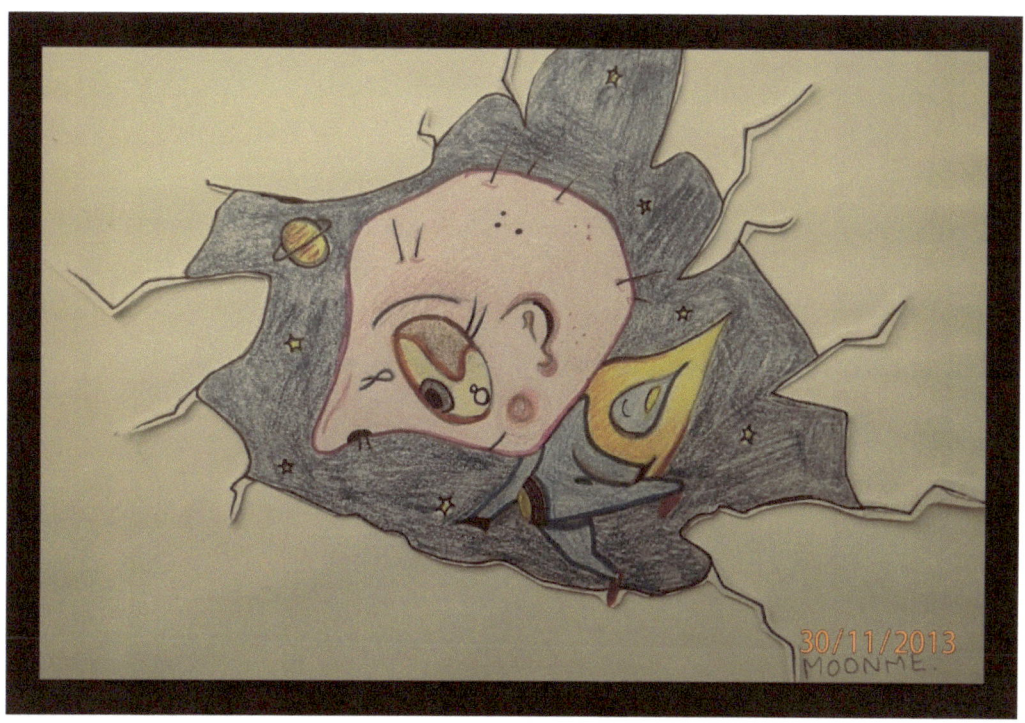

A superhero coming to save the earth!

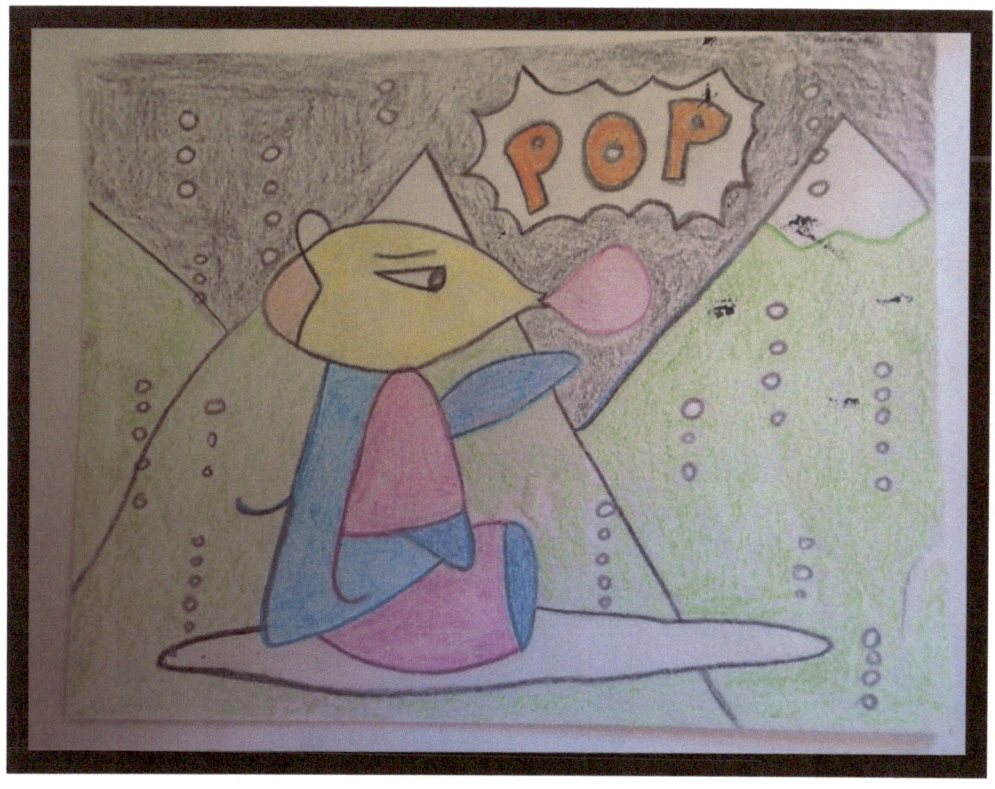

And a bubble-gum chewing earth representative goes to meet him.

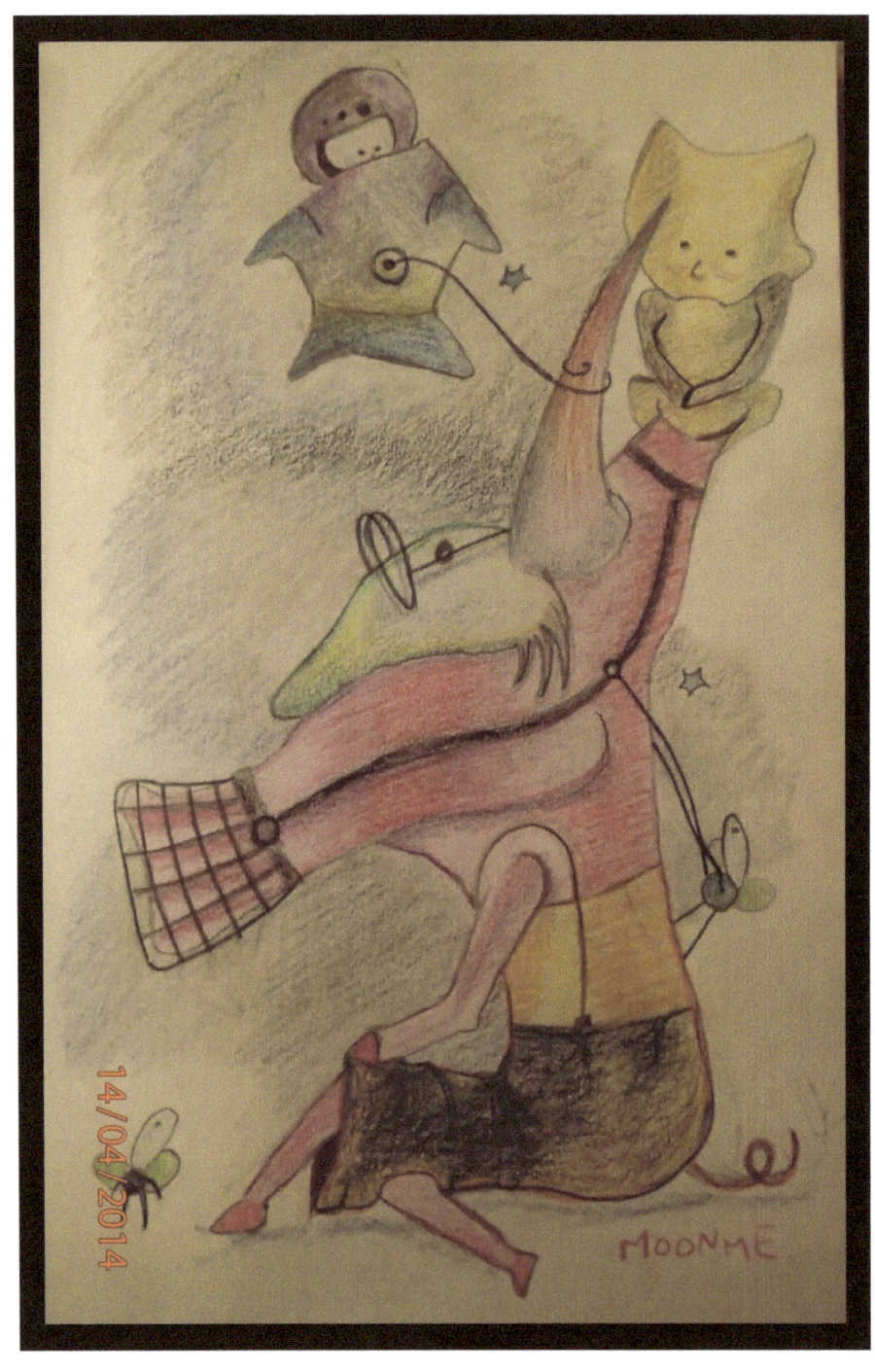

Now this one I don't like. Can you figure out why?

It's not really for any good reason, but I do not like the pig (I think she is a pig) in the middle of the picture. Do you like her?

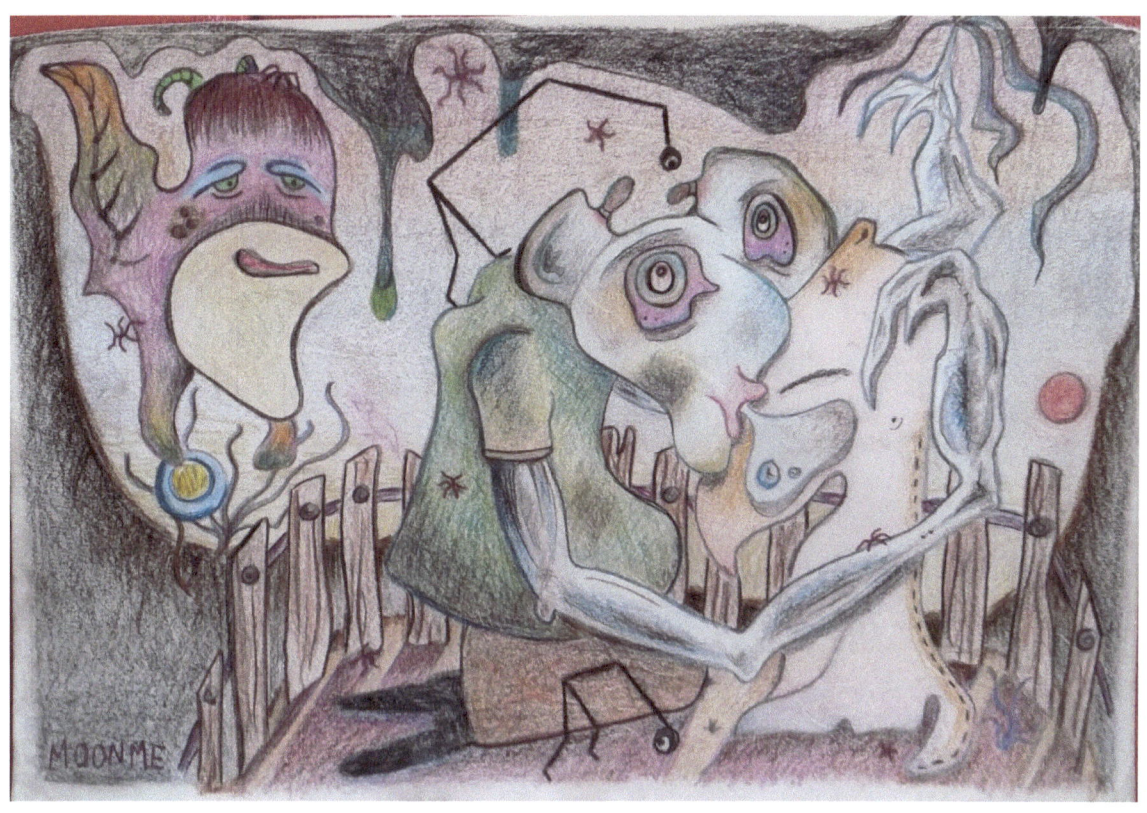

What do you see now?

Guess what, I see more bubble-gum! A man is giving his friend a hug and is blowing a big bubble over his eye. I hope he doesn't get groovy grape in his eyelashes.

The creature who is flying seems to have a Frisbee, but the others look a bit busy. Maybe the eyes on stalks will have a game, but how will they catch it?

Frisbee man may just have to wait.

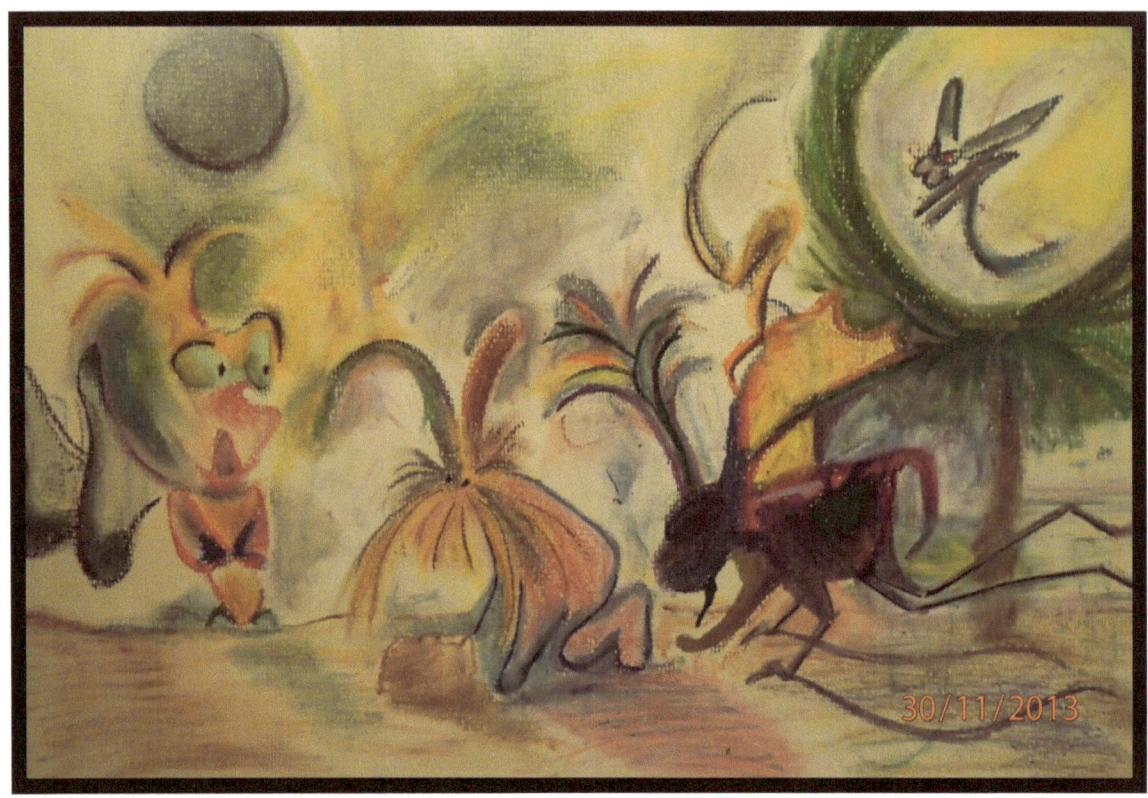

I see something strange in this one.

The two characters in the centre of the picture (one with a long moustache and the other with colourful horns) are bowed down in front of another character, who looks a bit like he is shouting.

Maybe it is because they put his pet cat, Anakin, up in a tree. He doesn't look very happy!

Someone may have to climb up and get him.

Or just shake the biscuit box – all cats come running to that!

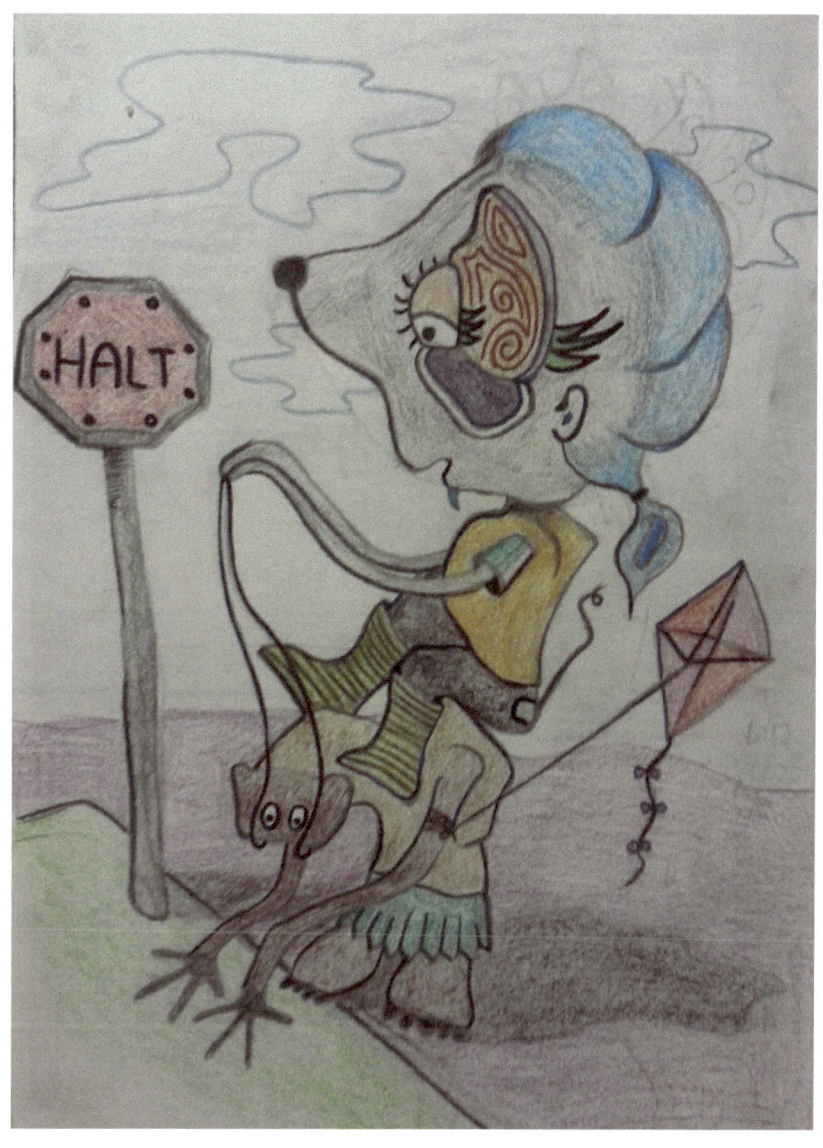

What do you think of this one?

I think the girl having a shoulder ride is very lazy, not only has she refused to walk, but she is making her transport hold the kite string! She must be heavy too, look at the size of her head!

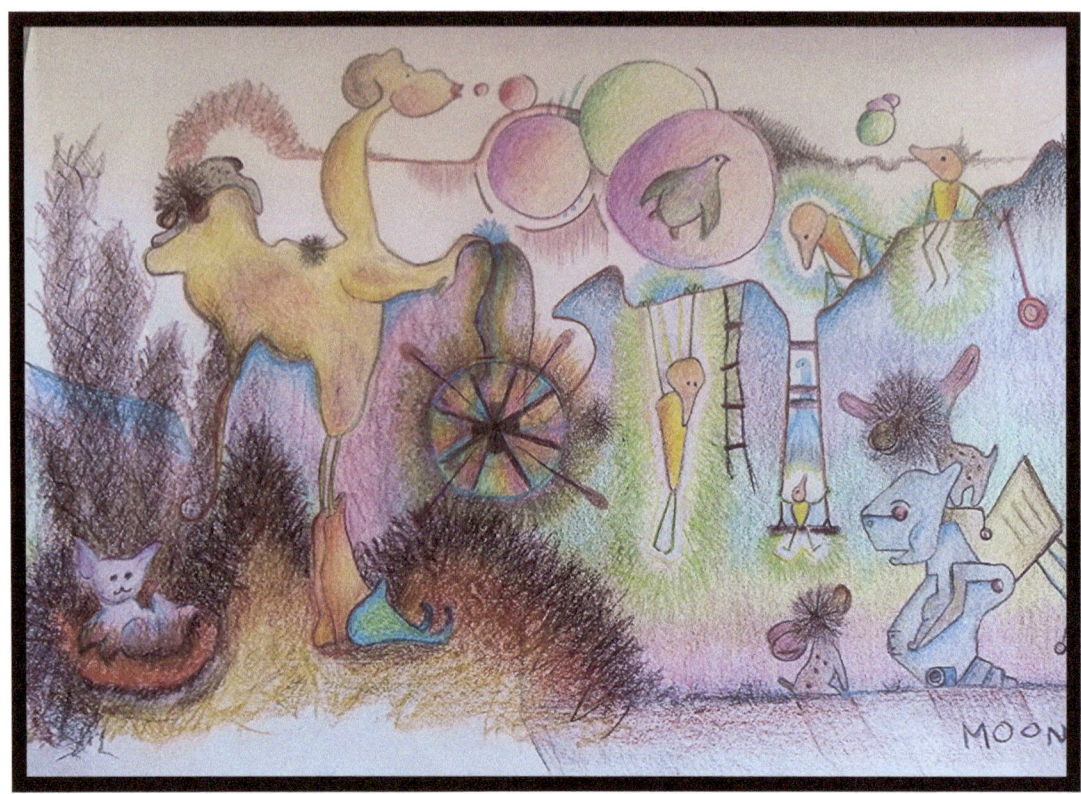

What do you see in this one? Can you count how many characters there are?

Can you spot the cat? Oh no, he is on fire!

What about the gorilla? He is playing with a yo-yo.

Can you find the robot? Some dogs seem to be trying to get him to play a game.

One more thing, can you spot the other yo-yo?

I found it!

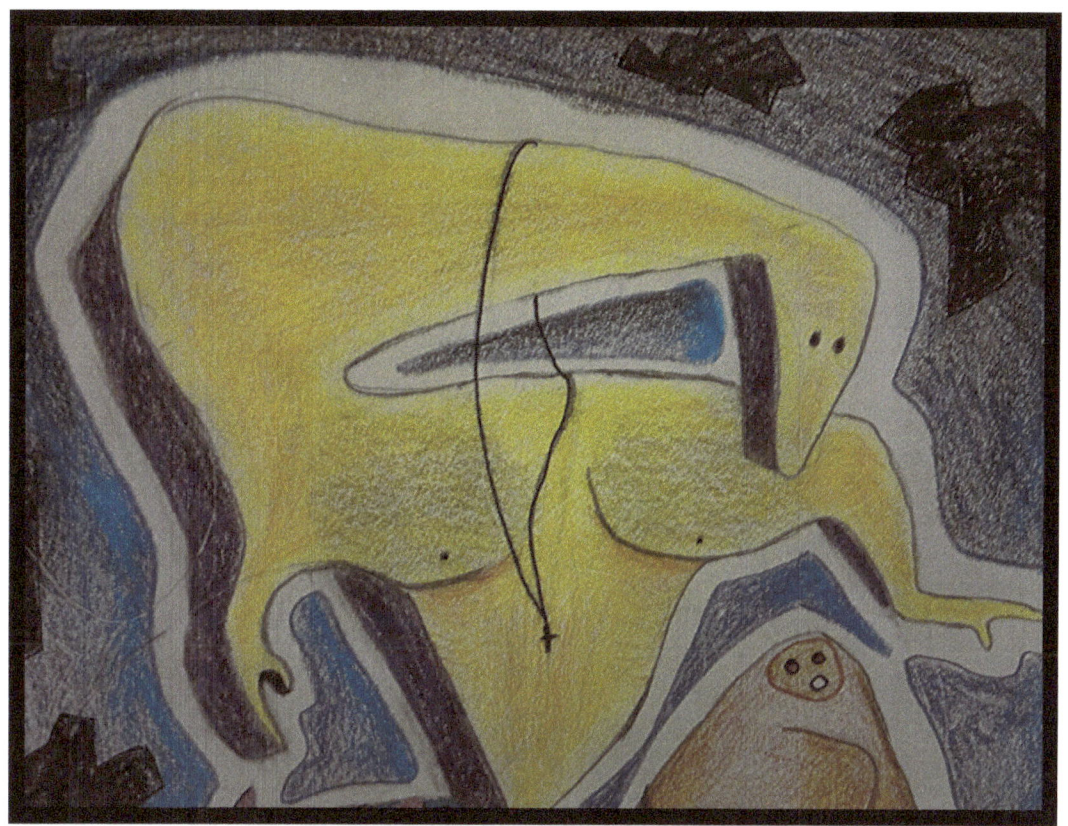

Look at the big, strong man. He is very muscly.

I think he is giving someone directions, I wonder where they are going.

He obviously likes jewellery too, he has a nice ornament on a long chain around his neck. Maybe he got that from his girlfriend last Christmas, or maybe he found it in the carpark.

It doesn't matter where it came from, it is very pretty.

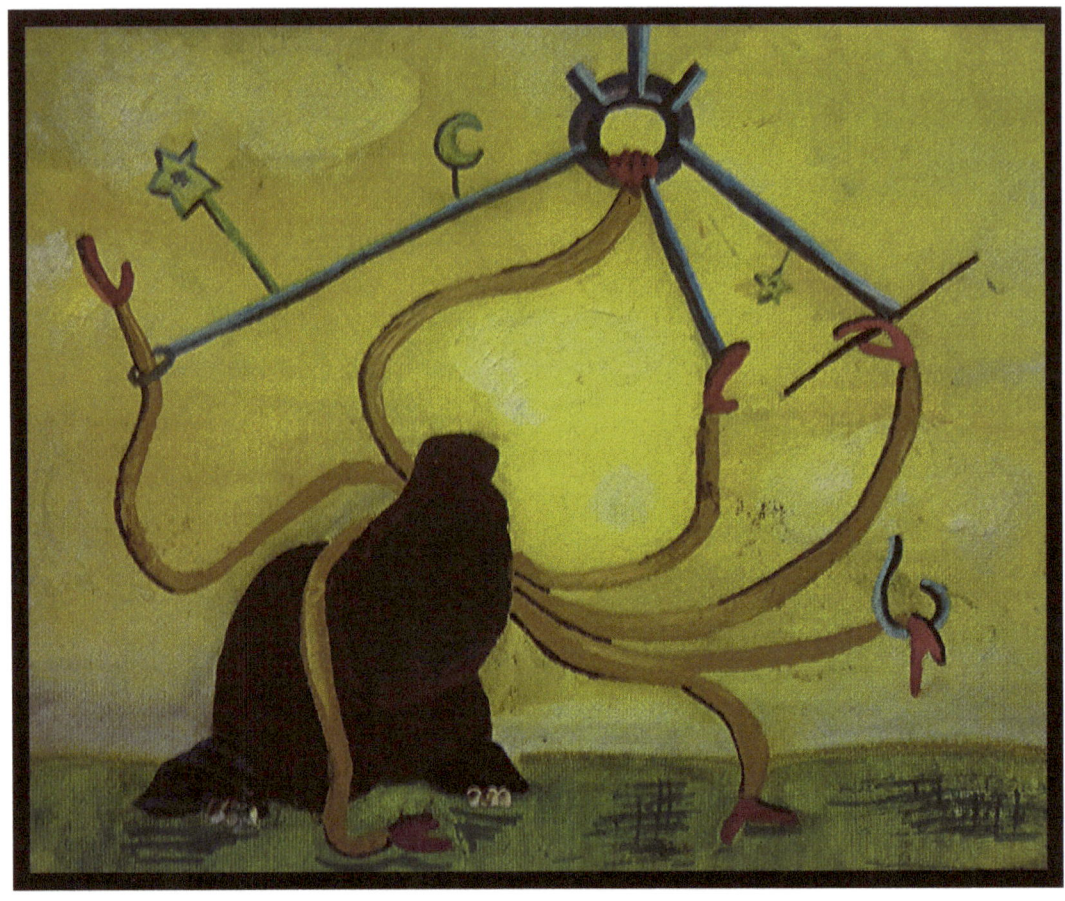

I have a question for you – what is the most annoying thing in the universe?

That's right! When you can't find the remote.

This character has evolved to have seven arms, in order to find the television remote more quickly.

I think it would be better if we evolved into creatures that didn't lose the remote in the first place.

I mean come on, he is clearly in the yard. Why would the remote be out there?!

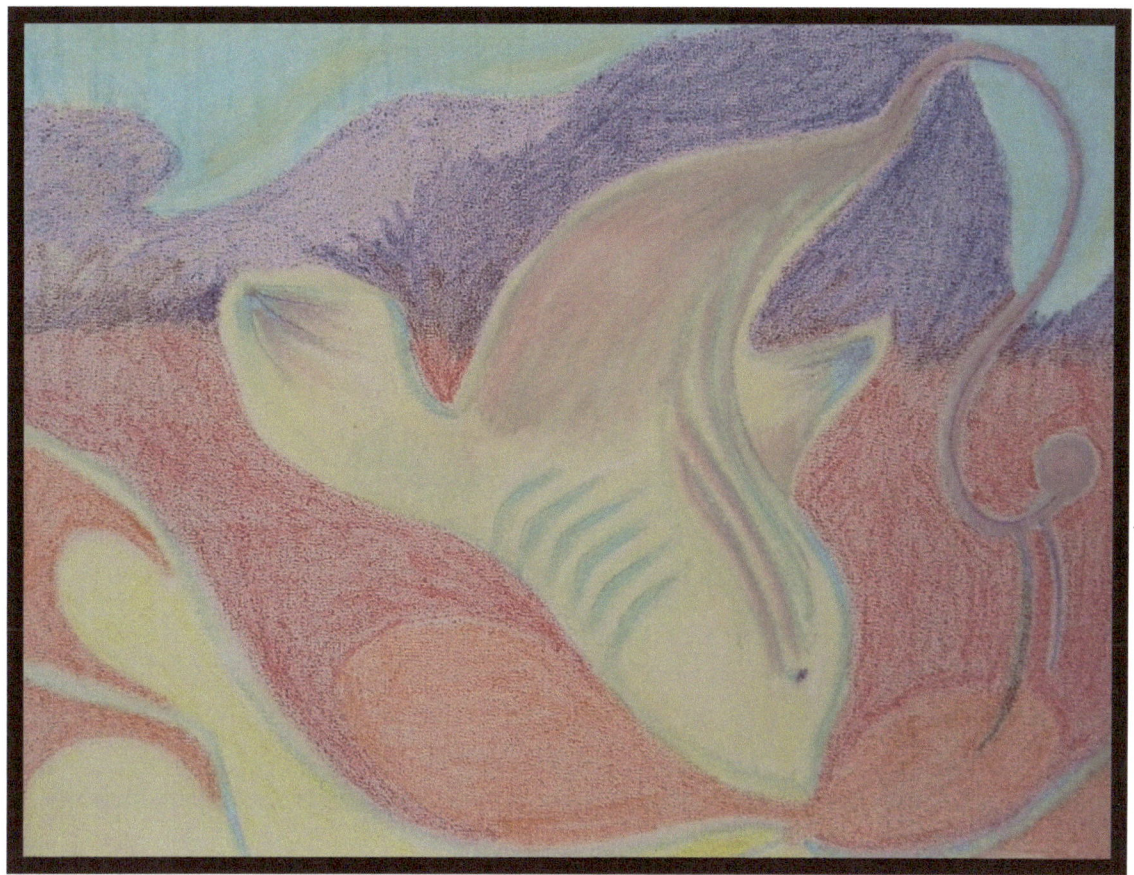

Now to me this is obvious, so I'll give you some clues:

1. The character is upside-down
2. He lives in the ocean
3. The world is also upside-down

Did you get it?

That's right it's a fish! With the purple ocean in the sky and the red sunset on the ground.

Can you see what he has on the end of his tail? It looks like some kind of sting. Do you think he is friendly?

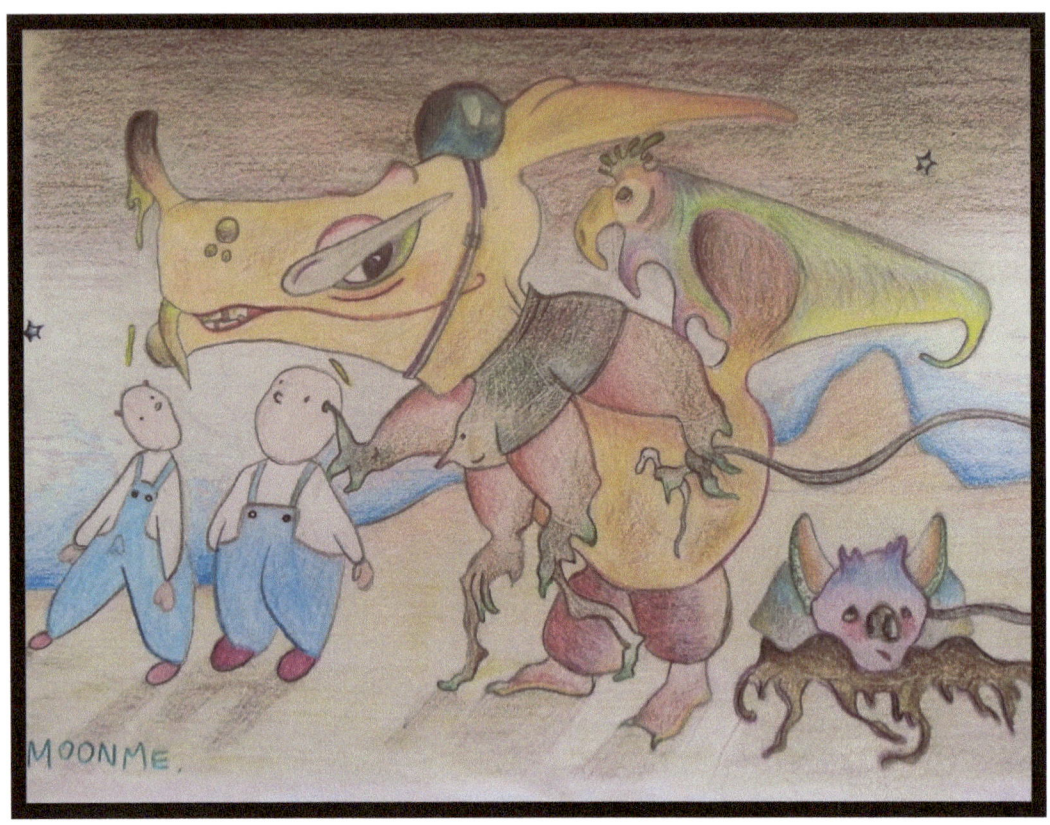

Well? What do you see now?

I see a dragon, who has a parrot attached to his bottom, and who is sticking his finger into the left ear of one of his companions. He holds in his hand a lead, which is attached to the collar of a spider, which has the face of a pig and the ears of a bat.

Bit of a weird picture really.

Would you stick your finger in someone else's ear? I wouldn't.

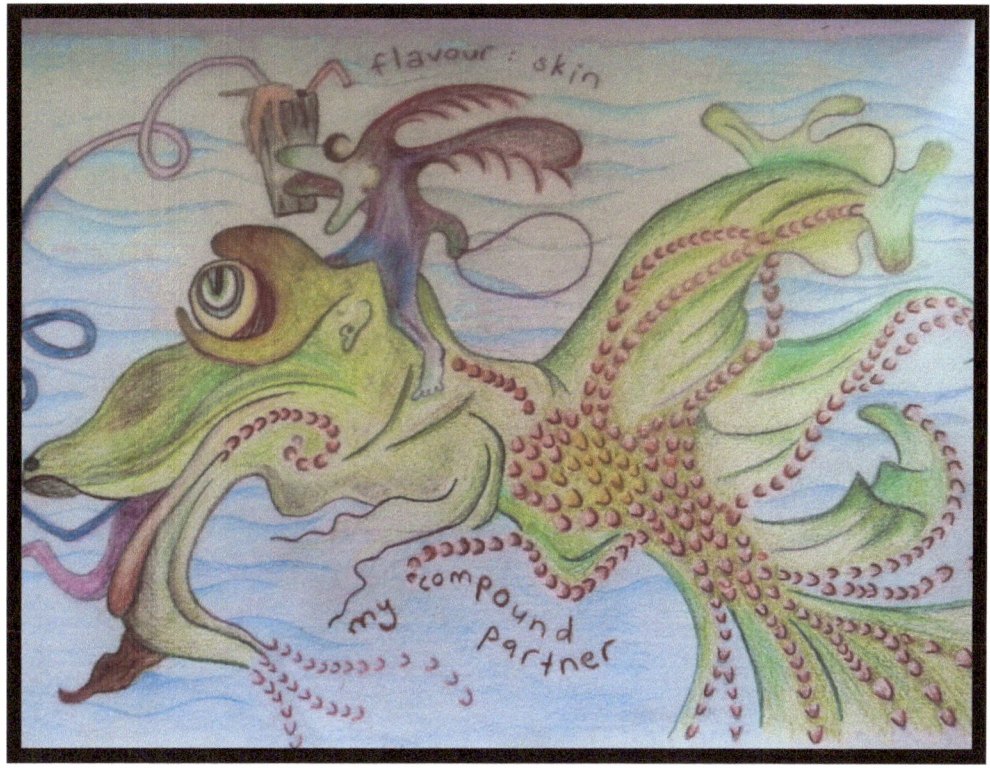

It's another dragon! This time he is flying.

He is very beautiful, can you see his scales? What colour are they?

The person riding on his back must be very brave, he doesn't even have a seatbelt!

What is that he is drinking? A skin flavoured milkshake?

Yuck!

I once had a dream where I was taken to a place where the meals were very strange, and I didn't want to eat or drink any of it. A skin flavoured milkshake was on the menu, along with ankle pie and shoulder stew.

It wasn't a nice dream!

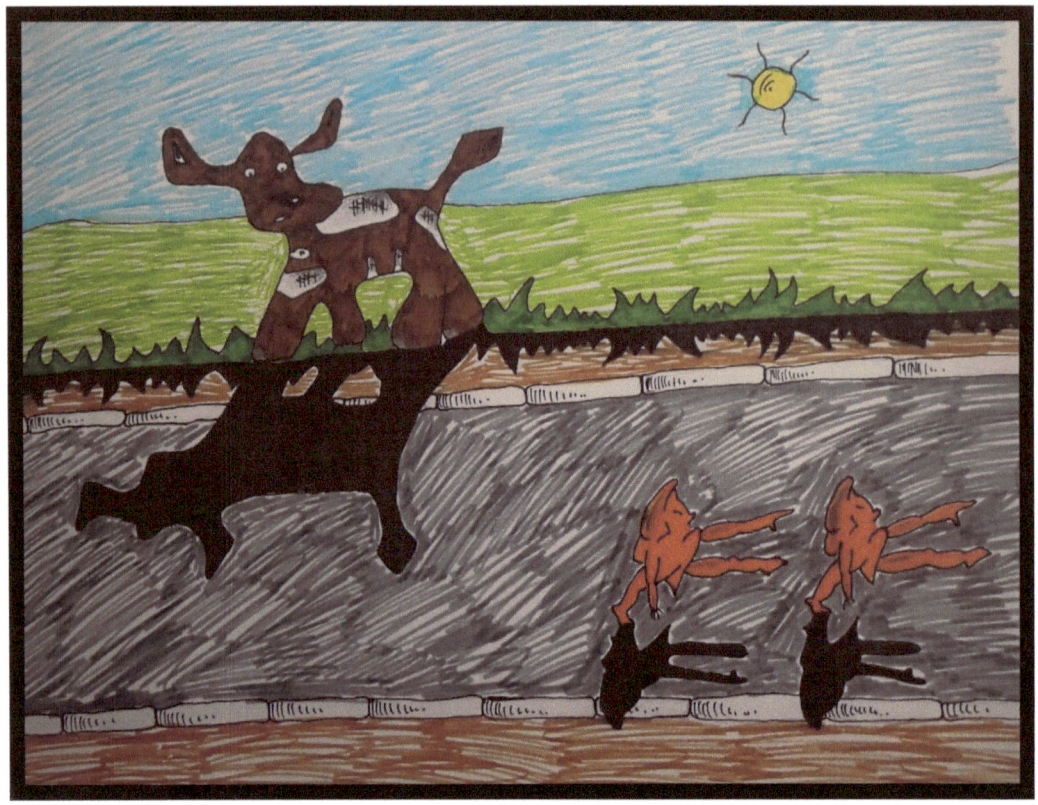

What do you think is happening here?

How about I tell you what was meant to happen here. You see the orange characters marching down the road? What do you think they are?

They actually are.....you'll never guess......two sausages! They don't look like sausages do they?

This might be why the dog looks so startled, he doesn't know what they are.

If they did look like sausages, what do you think he'd do?

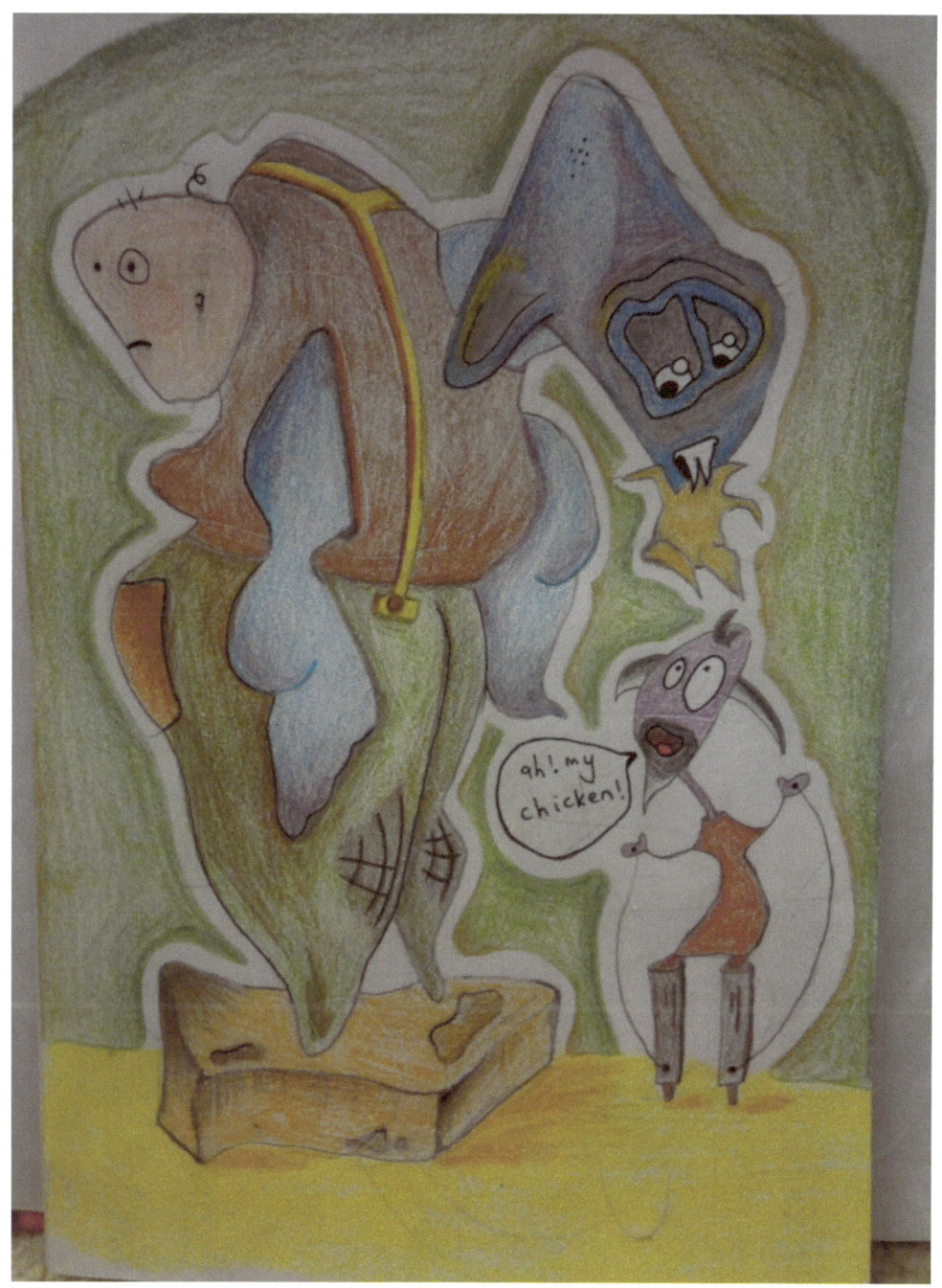

What do you see here?

Clearly the smaller character has lost a chicken, can you see where it is?

Here's a tricky question, how many heads can you see in the picture?

I can see three!

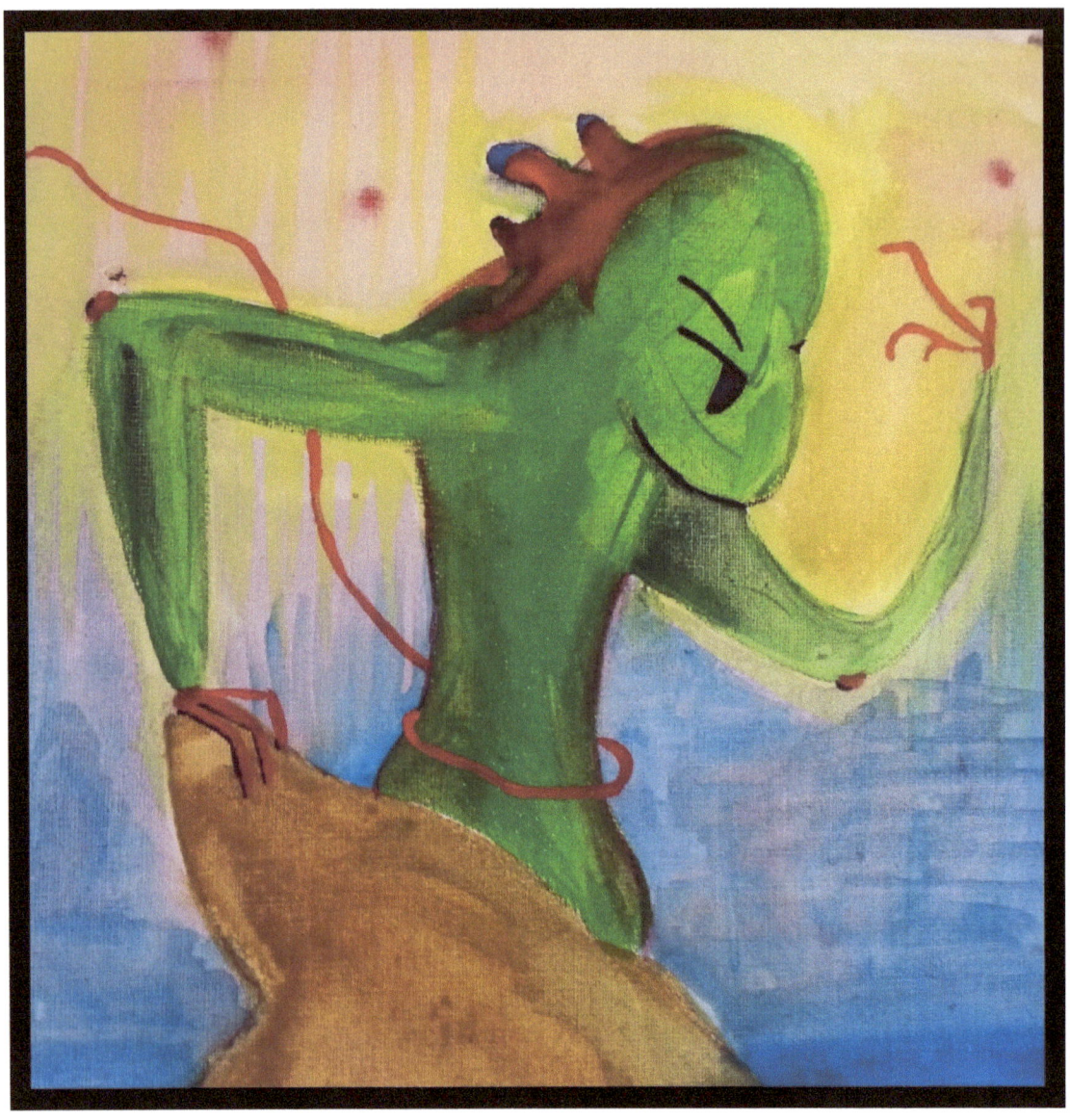

Who is this, and what are they doing? Tell me first.

I see a green lizard who is sitting on a rock in the ocean. He is upset about something and is yelling and making annoyed hand gestures at some poor soul.

What do you think he could be angry about?

Maybe he has lost his television remote.

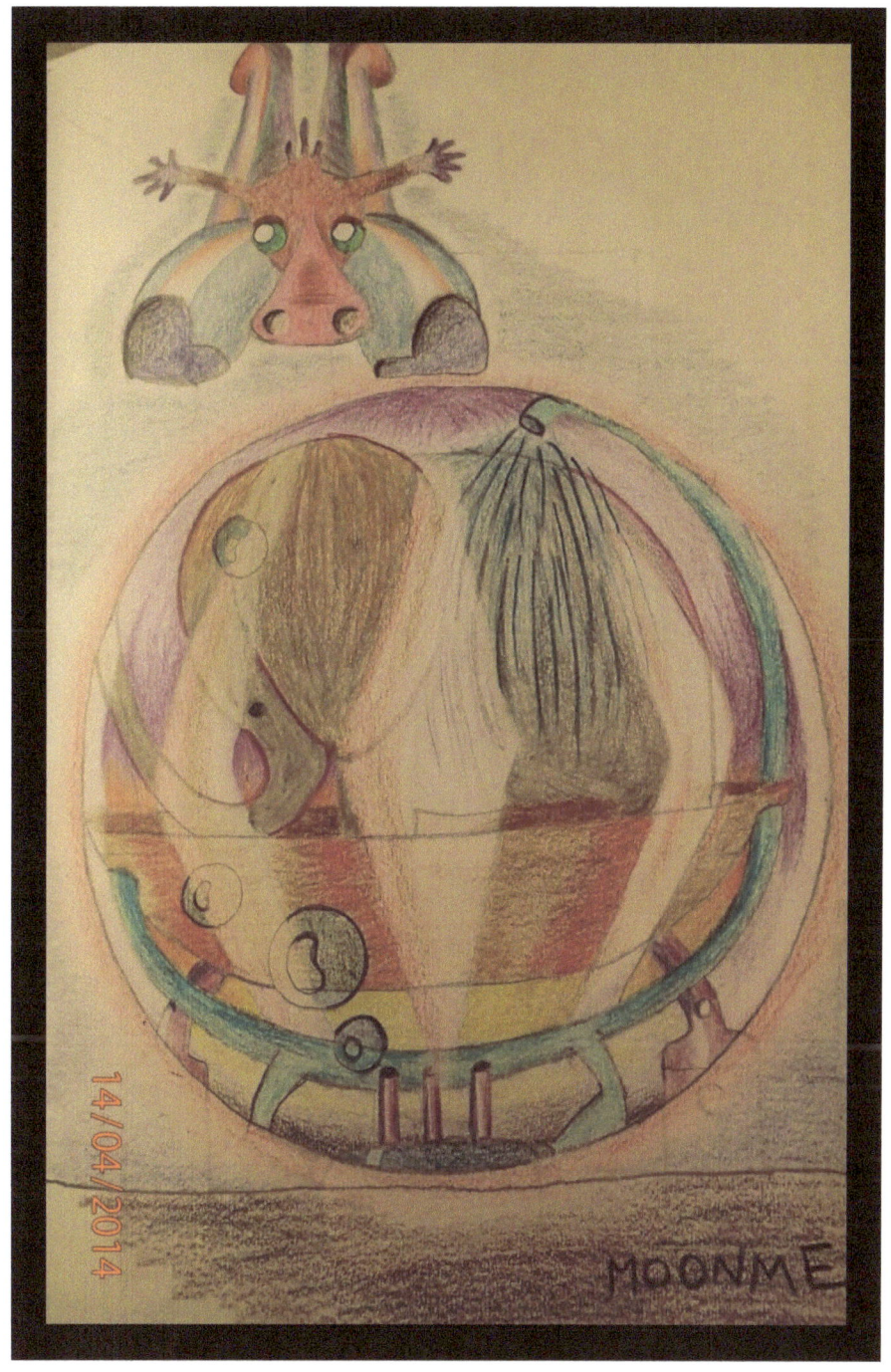

Can you guess what this elephant is trapped inside of?

That's right, a crystal ball!

He seems to be having a bath, it looks very cramped. Why would someone choose to take a bath inside a glass ball?

Someone is coming too, from up high. Better be quick, it's his turn!

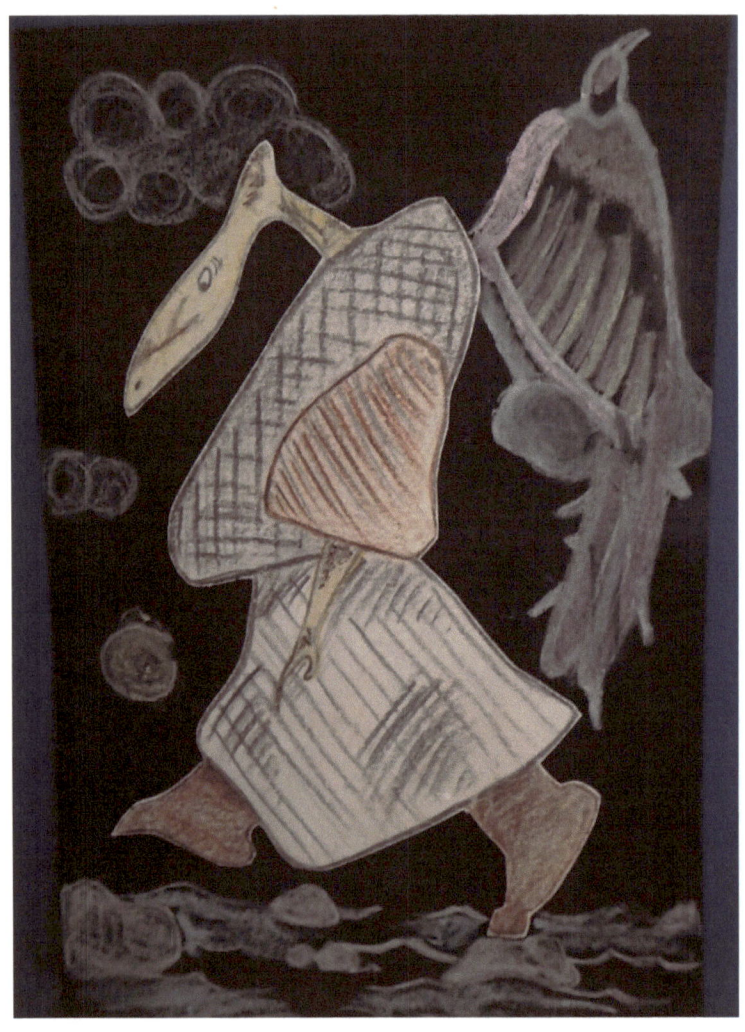

This guy actually has a name, can you guess it? It starts with an 'H',
and rhymes with Larry. He has a build-up of fines at a certain video
store. He finds it very difficult to part with rented movies.

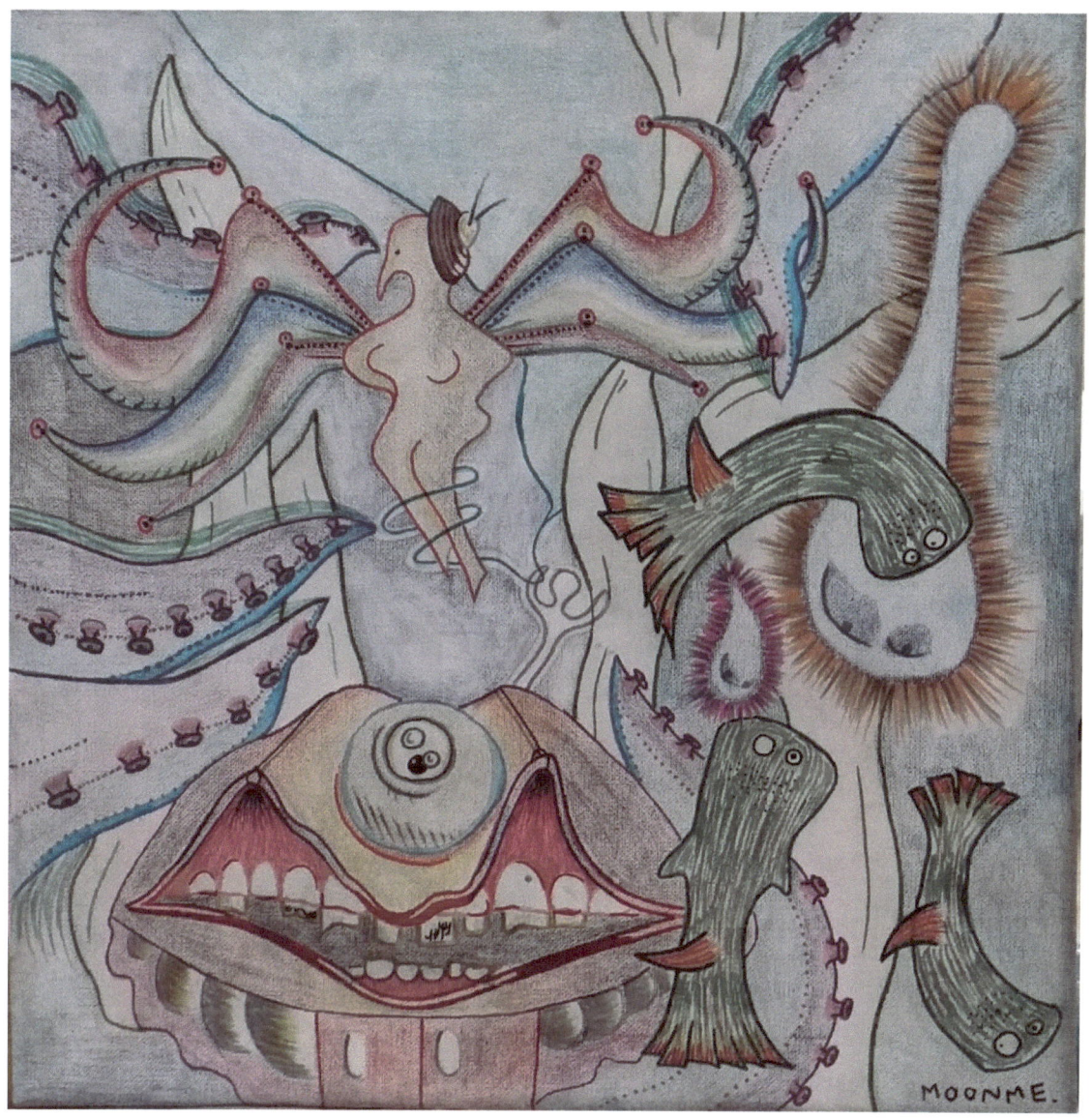

One last one, for good luck.

I can count seven characters in this picture, can you?

I see a clam getting ready for the dentist, a fairy floating about his head, three green fish with orange tails, and two blue creatures with fuzzy pink and orange scales.

Did you find them all? You are very clever.

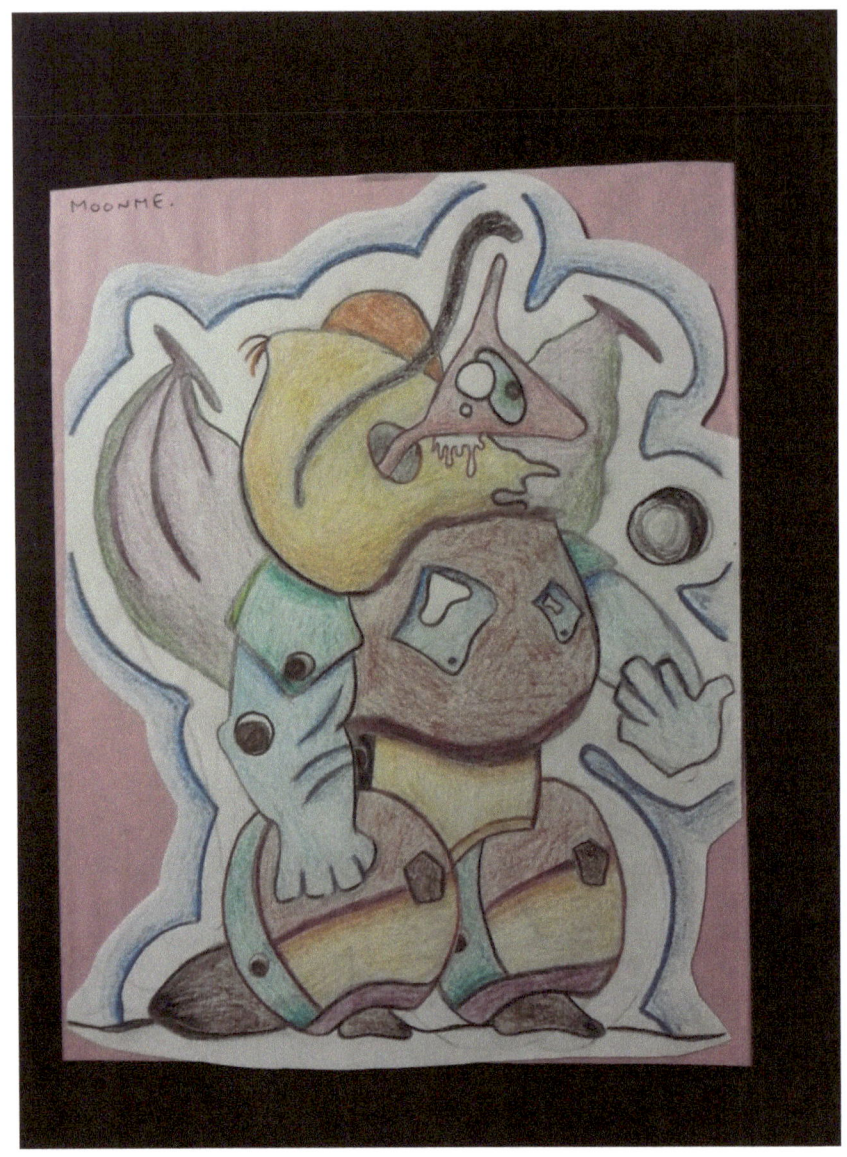

What do you think this guy does for a job?

I think he's a guard, that's why he wears a lot of armour.

He'll be in trouble if he ever needs glasses though, his eyeball looks like it is trying to escape!

Well? Did you see what I saw? Or did we see different things?

The way you see the world is probably very different to the way I see the world, so that's why what might look like a camel to me looks like a washing machine to you!

All very well if I was trying to draw a washing machine, but if I was actually trying to draw a camel I might need to take some art classes!

You can create any character you want, there are no rules.

And if you don't like how it turns out? Blame your pencil.

www.ingramcontent.com/pod-product-compliance
Lightning Source LLC
Chambersburg PA
CBHW050423180526

45159CB00005B/2388